I Grew Up
Playing With
Red Flags

I Grew Up Playing With Red Flags

Christine Zangrillo

Xlibris
1-888-795-4274
www.Xlibris.com

815286

CONTENTS

Dedication

This book is for my big hearted warriors. People tried to make you think that you were weak for being sensitive. They told you never to show your tears in public. They convinced you that you deserved the pain you felt. They convinced you that you were to blame for ignoring the signs. They didn't understand how love blinds us. They didn't understand that our ability to always look for the good in people is still a strength. Our golden hearts put us at a greater risk for deception, but they allow us to love deeply. It is why we are so compassionate, caring, and giving. The world would be much darker if our glittering golden hearts were locked away.

We've spent too long thinking we were weak for feeling. We were the brave ones. To let yourself feel and be vulnerable is greater strength than having a heart of stone. Our hearts are made of glass, but even broken glass can sparkle in the sun.

I want to thank my parents for their unconditional love and support for all of my aspirations. I want to thank my twin sister Jessie for showing me that we all have the potential to accomplish things we never thought we could. I want to thank my grandparents for always believing in me. I want to thank my best friends, Colleen, Erin, Jackie, Melanie, and Melissa for always being there for me. Lastly, I want to thank the men who have misused or abused my heart. You've not only inspired my poetry, but you also helped remind me that it is better to have loved and lost than to have never loved at all.

Introduction

I grew up playing with red flags. I played soccer for many years and it was pretty common to see red flags on the field. I also played capture the flag, where the sole object of the game was to go after that red flag and bring it back to your base at all costs. Little did I know that it would cost my heart a lot to play with red flags off the field.

Isn't red the color of passion and romance? Do people always stop at red lights and red stop signs? Despite the sign telling us to stop, we're not always inclined to do just that. Maybe you were distracted that day, and didn't see the warning sign. Maybe you saw the sign, but you were in a rush. You didn't want to bother worrying about the potential danger. Maybe you thought that you could reach the destination you desperately sought without suffering any damage. Maybe you ran one too many red lights...Now you're paying for all the times you ignored those glaring red signs.

-Her favorite color was red

You saw him wearing red,
Yet you couldn't keep him out of your head.
They should have taught you in gym class.
He's not the red flag you want to capture.
He lied once or twice,
Yet you still threw the dice.
They should have taught you in gym class.
He's not the red flag you want to capture.
You've always played games well.
It was hard to tell, that he was a heaven so close to hell.
They should have taught you in gym class.
He's not the red flag you want to capture.
His words and actions don't add up anymore.
Why don't you let him walk out the door?
They should have taught you in gym class.
He's not the red flag you want to capture.
You saw him wearing red,
Yet you couldn't keep him out of your head.
You'll be the one to blame if you keep playing this game.
Your harmonic heart will never sound the same.

Like my first book, *My Origami Heart,* the chapters of this book will be personal accounts of past relationships incorporated with my original poetry. These are real life experiences, involving real people. Once again, the names of the men have been changed for privacy reasons. Unlike my last book, not all of the chapters will be in the order of when I met the particular men mentioned.

Chapter One

Love Isn't Always Enough

Aiden. Where to begin? Right before Aiden came into my life, this hopeless romantic (me) felt pretty damn hopeless. I was so tired of building connections just for them to fall apart. As fate would have it, I became part of a new engagement group by the end of November 2017. I was 23 years old. It was an Instagram group made for liking and commenting on each other's posts. Was Aiden active on Instagram? Was he in the group? Nope. His sister was.

Our Instagram group began to infiltrate the real world when we all formed a group text chat. We even gave each other silly nicknames. Mine was unicorn. You'll understand why very soon. We decided to meet up for brunch. It was pretty cool to meet some of my online friends in person. After talking with me and meeting me at the brunch, Aiden's sister asked me if I might be interested in her older brother. I guess she figured nice, loyal, virgin girls were as rare as unicorns.

The first week of December, Aiden texted me for the first time. The conversation flowed easily. However, there was a pretty big obstacle between us. Over a hundred miles. He lived in a different state and the drive without traffic is about 3 hours long. To my surprise, that did not stop his enthusiasm to meet me. We quickly made plans to meet that upcoming weekend. Seven days after we started talking, we met for the first time. Despite a crazy snow storm brewing, Aiden drove to my house with his dog and got to meet my parents and sister. Not your typical first date, but it was perfect. He had brought two beautiful roses. He was very charming and made me laugh...A LOT.

As we stood outside in my yard with his arms around me, I kept wishing he would kiss me. It just felt like the perfect moment with the snow softly falling down. Later that evening when I made a joke about his dog kissing me first, I finally got my wish. Even though we weren't outside with the snow falling down, our first kiss felt magical. There was no denying the chemistry between us.

By the end of the weekend, I couldn't stop myself from basically asking that three word phrase most men cringe at hearing: "what are we?" I felt silly for "rushing" things so quickly, but it felt so right. We were acting like a couple, why not add the title? For the record, he agreed to the boyfriend and girlfriend label.

Three weeks later, late at night, Aiden and I were lying in bed talking about who knows what. We loved to have random deep conversations at bedtime. That was when he asked if he could tell me something he hadn't told anyone in a long time. When I said yes, he hesitated at first, but then said what I was already feeling in my heart: "I love you". I knew then that it wasn't just me. We both fell hard and fast for each other. Some might even call it love at first sight.

Your eyes are pristine windows gazed through.
Your heartbeat is rhythm danced to.
Your smile is light in all rooms entered.
Your embrace is relief after a long day.
Your touch is warmth craved after frostbite.
Your voice is melodious music on repeat.
Your essence is sweet honey on a Sunday morning.
Home is not a place.
Home is you.

To Aiden:

I'll never forget the first weekend we spent together at your place. We ordered Chinese and my fortune was quite telling. As you sat across from me, I read my fortune: "The love of your life is sitting across from you". I felt that I had never read a more accurate fortune. However, a darker fortune was also expressed later on during that weekend.

We were once again lying in bed. You randomly said that you were afraid you were going to mess things up between us. When I tried to ask you why, you didn't really have an answer for me. It would take a few months for your fear to come to light.

I truly thought love could conquer all. I had never been so in love, and I felt as if nothing could get in the way of us. I saw the good in you. I could feel the love in you. We shared so many special moments.

However, a few months into the relationship the red flags started to appear. I discovered things I did not know about you. Things I think you were trying to hide from me and yourself.

Despite the toxic turns, I held on tightly to the belief that we were one turn away from you being the man you wanted to be and told me you could be. I did whatever I could to support you. I knew relationships were supposed to be hard and I still believed our love could conquer anything.

Sadly, after being together for a year and a few months, things began to take an even darker turn. I was full of fear for the future of our relationship.

I light myself on fire to keep warm in a world so cold.
I sever my mind open to give the chaos room to breathe.
I close my eyes only to drown in the depth of my unconsciousness.
The brightest eyes hold the darkest secrets.
Silence gives voice to irreconcilable ideas.
If you find the real me, does that mean I was lost?
Tattoo your soul on my skin so mine can sit still.
It is good to be alone, but not lonely.

To Aiden:

Your marijuana addiction was getting harder and harder to deal with. I was so tired of coming in second to weed. You never saw it that way, but it was always a higher priority than me. You kept making promises you couldn't keep. Whether or not you truly wanted to quit, you could never follow through. It was so hard to know that you could look me straight in the eyes and lie to me about it.

From being a social worker/therapist, I knew the kind of control addiction has on people. I knew logically, that your smoking and lying did not mean that you did not love me. It just meant that you did not want to change. You were not ready to truly commit to transforming yourself and your life. I also knew that it wasn't just an addiction we were dealing with. I knew it was much deeper than that.

You also had a lot of anger in your heart. When it came out through road rage, it terrified me. You would be so quick to escalate situations instead of letting things go. However, that wasn't the scariest part. The moments when you would tell me that you would only be happy when you were dead and how you couldn't stop thinking of ways to kill yourself scared me the most. Time and time again, you would tell me how much you hated yourself and your life. Every negative word you said about yourself felt like a knife being dragged across my heart.

-A poem I wrote to you when you listed all the things you hated about yourself

I wish you could love yourself like I love you.
When I see your eyes, I see miracles of blue.
When you smile, the world glows.
Your hands are a sign of dedication, perseverance, and strength.
Your body is a work of art that houses your unique soul.
The world was not always kind to you.
That does not mean that you aren't worthy of kindness and love.
Don't be so hard on yourself when you fall.

Falling hurts enough as it is.
We are all human just trying to solve this puzzle of life.
The bravest of hearts have faced the most darkness.
There is light in you.
The world may try to blow out your flame, but you are more powerful than you know.
When you channel your mind toward your inner light, you will be unstoppable.
You can't stop someone who refuses to give up.
You can be the sun.
You may feel that you are sinking, but you always rise back up.

You were so depressed and full of self-loathing, but refused to seek counseling and get help. What more can you do when the one you love is suffering, but refuses to do anything about it?

-I loved you so much that I felt your pain as if it were my own

Some days my skin glows in the warmth of your smile.
Other days my heart sinks to the bottom of the ocean floor.
Your despair and pain became chains to my ankles dragging me down.
In your sorrow I began to drown.
I choke on the venomous words you shoot at yourself.
Your demons drag their claws across my skin.
They sink their fangs into my mind.
I'm lost in your darkness.
I feel, but I cannot see.

I thought a break would be good for us. I did not see it as the end of our love story. I thought the time and space would allow you to see what truly mattered to you. I thought it would bring you back to me.

Only a few days into the "break" you decided that you could not give me what I needed. You decided that you did not care about your mental health and did not want to try to quit smoking either. I was devastated. At the time, I felt like you had given up on us too quickly, but I guess you also felt that by asking for a break I had already given up too. I just did not see that coming.

-I never wanted to leave

I put on a brave face,
But I've never felt so out of place.
I try so hard to be strong,
But this all feels so wrong.
We were never good at goodbye.
Maybe that's why I still cry.
I walked away,
Even when my heart said stay.
That was the hardest thing I've done to this day.

Although we were "broken up", we couldn't bear to be out of complete contact for too long. I think the longest we went with zero communication was around a week. It seemed we both yearned to be back together, but knew that nothing was really resolved. Fate, however, had other plans.

A couple weeks after the break up, I went to an Avatar conference for the weekend. It is basically a program that involves a lot of introspection. It helps you uncover your underlying beliefs, notice patterns in your life, and how your beliefs influence your experiences. I did this program in hopes of "finding myself" so to speak. I knew the event took place in Aiden's state of residence, but I did not anticipate any connection between the location and Aiden since the town was about an hour away from him. When I arrived, I recognized the area. At first I couldn't figure out why. Then it hit me. I had been in that exact area before with

Aiden. What are the odds? Being me, the hopeless romantic, I took it as a sign that we would cross paths again. The universe was not going to let me forget about him that easily.

To Aiden:

I'll never forget when you called me the last week of May 2019. It had been over a month since we had seen each other and almost just as long since the break-up. You said that you had been on your way to surprise visit me when you got into a terrible car accident. You were hit from behind by a box truck, sending your car on top of the highway median. You had somehow managed to be unscathed physically, but mentally you were transformed. Your whole outlook on life had changed. You told me how you realized that you had been too comfortable living a negative life. You were ready to do and be better. Although your car ended up getting totaled, everything seemed to work out the way it should. We face-timed that night for a few hours like old times. You convinced me to drive to you the next morning.

You said that you were quitting smoking for good and agreed to join an online mental health support group. Since you seemed to be finally making the big changes I needed from you, I agreed to get back together.

When I saw you, I felt like my heart was going to explode from happiness. Spending that weekend with you I could feel the changes already. Your energy had completely shifted. You seemed so much calmer, more patient and positive. It was like you had reached a new level of peace.

In November 2019, a month shy of our two year anniversary, I reflected on our time together. I have experienced the most love and pain ever in my life within these two years. I have no regrets. I told myself that love should be put to the test. I thought that love does not need to be perfect, it just needs to be true, and I had never loved someone the way I loved Aiden.

I thought back to all the little moments where you made me feel so loved and cared for. Whenever I would freak out about my weight or not want to go somewhere without makeup on, you would always tell me how I'm perfect the way I am and how beautiful I am naturally. Even when I didn't say anything, you would randomly tell me how beautiful I looked first thing in the morning.

When we were walking your dog, you picked that pretty purple flower and put it in my hair. Another time you picked white flowers for me. I also remember when you surprised me with beautiful red and orange roses when we were reunited after my Disney trip. You had no idea how much those seemingly small gestures meant to me.

Another time, you had found strings in the shape of a dumbbell and immediately thought of me since you know how I like to work out at the gym. I always kept it attached to my car key ring.

Another time, you were going to use a coin, but decided to save it for me. The coin had horses on it and you knew how much I love horses.

Sometimes I've tried to order new food and did not like the result. You've always been willing to trade with me or give me some of your food.

I'll never forget when we were in Florida, we went out to eat with my family for my mom's birthday. I was really looking forward to getting a drink, but I had left my ID at the hotel room. The waitress said that if I could at least produce a picture of my driver's license, she would be able to get me a drink. You took the time to scroll through hundreds of photos on your phone to find the picture of my license I had sent to you when I got it renewed. You were so determined to find the photo for me. Many scrolls later, your search proved successful. You were my hero that night. It might seem silly to some people, wondering what is the big deal about being able to have one drink or not, but it's the principle of it. You saw that I was disappointed and you did everything you could to make me feel better.

Another memory that sticks out to me is one time in the evening. We had said our usual "goodnight" and "I love you" over the phone before going to bed. You called me back shortly afterward saying, "I don't know if I told you already, but I love you". I thought that was so sweet that you called me back just to make sure you told me that.

Whenever we would go anywhere, you always held my hand. Holding your hand always brought me comfort and peace. It's those little moments where you might start to walk ahead of me, but then reach your hand back, waiting for me to take it that melted my heart.

Despite all the beautiful moments we shared, there were just as many ugly moments. It was as if when things were good between us, it felt like heaven on Earth. I felt like I was higher than cloud nine. Nothing felt more right. But when things were bad, it felt like hell on Earth. There was no greater pain and despair. The moment you told me that I said "I love you" too much. The moment you told me that true love no longer existed between us. The moment you said that me wanting you to quit smoking caused your love for me to fade. The moments when you made me feel weak and overly sensitive when I would cry in front of you. Moments like those cut me to the bone. It was like dating Dr. Jekyll and Mr. Hyde. Sometimes when I would come see you, I never knew who was going to greet me.

The drastic changes that I saw in you when we got back together slowly seemed to fade. That online support group you joined? You never utilized it, not even once. When I visited you in December for Christmas, I had a bad feeling and looked through your phone. Once again you tried to lie to my face. After much persistence, you finally admitted that you had started smoking again behind my back. You said this has been going on without my knowledge for two months. For all I know, it could even be longer. It absolutely shattered me. I value honesty above everything else. Without trust, how can a relationship survive? We had a long talk, and I thought we were on the same page.

Sadly a week later, more lies were said and I reached my breaking point. I knew I would be enabling unless I ended the relationship. I had run out of options. I thought my heart broke the first time you ended our relationship, but this was an entire new level of shattered. Even though it was my choice, it did not make it any easier. So many times after, I questioned my decision. How could a love so strong not be enough to save this relationship?

It all feels like a nightmare.
The thought of us ending is too much to bare.
I just feel so alone.

It cuts me to the bone.
It's driving me crazy not to call you on the phone.

-"Break or Bend"

There is a hole inside of me I can't fight off.
No matter what I do,
All I see is you.
I try to act like it's all okay,
But I fall apart every day.
How did the most beautiful love story fade from me?
Part of me still believes we're meant to be.
My heart just can't accept that this is the end.
Will the line I walk break or bend?

-Even though I left, you never left my mind

I think of you every day.
You have no idea how much I wanted to stay.
I can't bear to hurt anymore.
It feels like my heart and head are constantly at war.
After I pray,
I dream of all the things I wish I could say.
I try to run from my mind,
Because I'm terrified of what I'll find.
I'll be forced to face what I had tossed.
So much has been lost.

Anyone who has ever been in love knows just how difficult it is for the heart to let go of a vision it believed in for so long. I spent over two years envisioning our future together. We talked about where we might live, what kind of house we would have, what we would name our kids...If you're anything like me, it is also hard to let go of a relationship that you've invested so much time and effort into. You literally went above and beyond to make it work. You emotionally and mentally exhausted yourself.

Growing up watching Disney movies and reading fairytales, I was surrounded by the idea that love was always enough. Despite all the odds stacked against them, no evil witch or wicked stepmother could keep the lovers apart. The prince rescued the princess and they lived happily ever after. Love always seemed to win in those tales. But what if true love isn't always enough? Those Disney movies and fairytales never showed what happens when mental illness or addictions infect relationships. They didn't show you how in real life you don't just one day live happily ever after without facing any more challenges. The real monsters don't have ugly faces and sinister laughs. They are the voices in your head telling you that you are unworthy of love and happiness. You see, in real life, you may find your "true love", but sometimes the monsters win. Darkness does not disappear just because you have fallen in love.

It was the hardest lesson I ever had to learn...Love alone is not enough to save a relationship. Just because you love someone, does not mean you should stay in a romantic relationship with them. For a relationship to survive and flourish, it needs honesty, communication, trust, equal effort, and compatibility. Although Aiden and I were not meant to stay in a relationship together, he will always hold a very special place in my heart.

Several months have passed since the breakup. Aiden and I still communicate and maintain a friendship. Not all breakups are fortunate enough to have this kind of outcome. I knew the moment we met that we had a special connection. Sure it's possible to connect with many souls, but never the same way twice. I can see now that we were meant to have the relationship we did when we did. We clicked in many ways, but not in enough ways for us to have a successful long term romantic relationship. It is like completing a puzzle with a missing piece. In many ways it looks great. It almost seems like a perfect completed picture, but something is off. Someday I will find someone who carries the piece Aiden and I were missing.

Chapter Two

Not All Clowns Wear Makeup

Isn't it funny how when you're in a relationship on Facebook you rarely get new friend requests? Yet when your status changes to single, the requests come pouring in! I swear within the first week of changing my Facebook status to single, I got over twenty new friend requests. Shocker- they were all from men. Seeing mutual friends, I accepted some, not thinking much of it. Eventually a guy I will refer to as Ryan sent me a message telling me how beautiful I am.

He seemed like a genuine guy at first, but don't they all? He didn't waste any time. He asked me my age and about my passion. Once the conversation shifted from Facebook messenger to text message, the red flags began to appear. He kept insisting that I come over to his house. Honestly a man asking to meet a girl for the first time at his house couldn't have been a bigger warning. That right there should have made me run for the hills, but he was very attractive and charming. Going through the hardest heart break of my life, I was extra vulnerable and he took advantage of that.

When I even tried to call him out about only being after one thing, he denied it. He told me how there was a chance that we would really hit it off in person and be married in several years. Let's not kid ourselves. He only said that to throw me off his trail.

He only wanted to see me after dark.
The narcissist wanted to leave his own mark.
Yet again I was so blind.
If only I could rewind.
Those pretty boys speak the most beautiful lies
While even looking you dead in the eyes.

Despite his begging, I could not be persuaded. I insisted that our very first meeting should be at a public place. After all, I didn't really know this guy. He could be a rapist or serial killer for all I knew. *Insert shrug shoulder emoji*

To Ryan:

Although you said you made good money with your job, you claimed you currently couldn't afford to go out to eat with me and that was your excuse for why we should just meet at your house. Red flag alert.

Since I really wanted to meet you, I told you I would pay for everything. Only then did you finally agree to meet me for sushi. I showed up a few minutes before our designated meeting time. You did not extend the same courtesy. You called me at that time just to tell me that you would be twenty minutes late. Yet again, another red flag.

When you did finally show up, you were just as charming and charismatic in person. The conversation flowed very easily. I should have known that since you were a salesmen, you were a professional bullsh*tter. You knew all the right things to say. As expected, I paid for both our meals.

After I got home, you texted me telling me how you really enjoyed meeting me. You suggested I even come over your house later that same night. What a surprise that you were already back to that topic…You were practically trying to wave the red flag in my face. I declined, but suggested we meet at my gym the next morning since we talked about training together. You ended up bailing on those plans.

-Why was I always so good at capture the flag

You were a walking red flag.
On our first date,
You were 20 minutes late.
Yet I paid, even though you made me wait.
Why did I ignore that flashing red sign?
I really wanted to believe your line.
I quickly became old news,
But damn, if you only knew you were going to lose.
You lost a heart of gold.
If only your soul wasn't so cold.

The next time, you followed through with plans. I lent you the book I wrote, *My Origami Heart*, because you said you wanted to read it. Maybe that was the greatest irony. You showed the same lack of respect and genuine interest for the book as you did for me and my emotional heart. Time would go by, and whenever I would text you and ask if I could have my book back, you would make up an excuse and insist that you hadn't had time to read it, but you still wanted to. After several failed attempts, you told me that you lost my book.

I thought I met a narcissist before,
But then you waltzed through a similar door.
You're used to having your own way.
You wouldn't listen to what I tried to say.
I knew your game,
So I should be the one to blame,
But it takes two to tango,
And you didn't have to stoop so low.

I couldn't believe that you somehow managed to lose my book. You claimed that you checked everywhere for it, even your car, but let's be real. We both know that book was never opened and never left your room. Surprisingly you did offer to replace it and even texted me the receipt from Amazon. The next day, however, you somehow managed to find it. You said it was shoved behind other books in your room. At first, you told me that you wanted me to give you back the new one you had ordered so that you could return it. God forbid you do anything extra for someone.

Beware a writer,
She'll bring your darkness to light.
She won't shy away from showing her scars.
You won't see her drowning her sorrows at the bars.
You left her to drown,
Not knowing she'd wear the damage like a crown.

After what felt like an eternity later, you finally stopped by my house one night to return my book. Although you had been previously avoiding me like the plague, you surprised me by trying to have a conversation with me. Instead of dropping off the book in my mailbox as you had planned to do multiple times before, you actually met with me face to face. You were wearing shorts since you came from the gym. Despite your shivering from the cold, you proceeded to ask me what was new with me and if I had any plans for the weekend. I couldn't believe how you were choosing now of all times, standing in shorts in the cold, to attempt to hold a conversation with me. You even told me that I should join you at a bar Saturday night if I didn't have plans. You told me to text you, but I didn't. I finally started fearing your flags. I didn't try to meet up with you that weekend.

I don't live a life of regret,
But damn, I'm sorry we met.
You casted baited hooks.
You were so used to using your looks.
I was tired of swimming and took your bait.
You could hardly wait to throw me on your polished plate.
I was unarmed,

And most vulnerable to be harmed.
You didn't care.
For you, it was a fun dare,
To capture a breed so rare.
Once you had your fill,
There was no more thrill.
You threw me back knowing I already had a wounded gill.

One time I texted you to confront you. I asked why you acted so into me and then ran for the hills. You tried to explain that you could see something with me, but you weren't ready for a relationship. You said that you knew I was a good girl and that you didn't want to hurt me. I'll never understand why men have this realization when it's too late and the damage is already done. On the plus side, you did decide to let me keep the copy of my book you ordered from Amazon. How chivalrous of you...

-The Devil was Once an Angel

Don't chase a pretty face.
He's a fallen angel unworthy of your saving grace.
He wants to fly on your wings,
But he's not the kind of man who believes in giving rings.
Despite your angelic glow,
He will eventually go.
He realizes he cannot keep you,
So he runs before you do.

-The words my heart screamed when you left

I'm so fed up with these clowns,
But they seem to be all over these towns.
I've met fake,
But you still take the cake.
You would always flake.
You only knew how to take.
You collect hearts just to make them break.
Why did you want to prick a heart like mine?
Do you always make a girl pay when you dine?
I should have taken notice of the sign,
That your intentions were anything but benign.
It is easy to take a man or woman with a good heart for granted.
We put in effort even if you don't.
We are always rooting for you.
We shower light and positivity on your darkest days because it is in our nature,
But our value doesn't lessen because we freely love and give.
Just as it is a privilege to wake every morning and bask in the rays of the morning sun,
It is a privilege to stand in the light of a good man or woman.

Chapter Three

A Red Flag Fortune

My family always had a gym membership, but it would take a long time for me to utilize it. This chapter unfolded the summer before I started college. I had never lifted before, but I knew I needed to learn because it was going to be part of my D1 track program for school. I was a sprinter and our coach wanted us to use weightlifting to improve our explosiveness. My mom promptly set up an appointment for me with a personal trainer at the gym to show me how all the equipment worked.

If you've read my book, *My Origami Heart*, you will remember a man I referred to as Cody. The person I will be talking about in this chapter is the "original Cody". You will find out why later on. I don't want to spoil anything and get ahead of myself.

When I first met Cody, I could tell he was very into bodybuilding. This man was jacked, but it was obvious that it was not natural. He later admitted to me that he took anabolic steroids. He was bald and had a tongue ring. I guess he took his job as a personal trainer very literally because he sure became overly personal. He was very flirtatious. I noticed my first red flag when I spotted the name of a girl tattooed on his wrist. He told me that it was an ex and that he was going to make an appointment to get it covered up.

Why did I ignore that flag tattooed on your skin?
You always lied about where you'd been.
You told me all the things I wanted to hear to keep away any fear.
You told me to meet you at a different gym.
You wanted us to go for a swim.
We hung out in the hot tub not having a care.
I should have known you wouldn't play fair.
You wanted to have your cake and eat it too.
I knew what I had to do.
I realized I was the side chick.
Men like you make me sick.

I think men forget that girls are basically FBI agents. Never underestimate a woman's ability to uncover the truth. I remember I was stalking Cody's Twitter and I came across a girl's account who had the same name as his wrist tattoo. It became apparent that this was no ex-girlfriend. It seemed that they were even living together. She had the same name as the girlfriend of Cody in my original book. You read that right. Two completely separate times in my life I was going on dates with someone who had the same name and both their secret girlfriends also shared the same name. This original Cody was a red flag fortune in disguise.

All by herself,
She ponders why history repeats itself.
So close to something great,
But yet again she must wait.
Maybe it's never the right time or the right one,
But she's not like the other girls looking for short lived fun.
She wants something real that will last.
She won't lose faith from the scars of her past.
No one will change her mind,
Because why be a copy when you can be one of a kind?
Go against the crowd,
Even if their voices seem loud.
Stay true to who you are,
And let your true essence shine as bright as any star.

To Cody:

Shortly after I found out about your secret girlfriend, you seemed to no longer be working at the gym. I assume you were fired quite frankly. I'm sure it was frowned upon to make out with clients at the gym facility. I probably wasn't the only personal training client you became overly personal with.

Years went by. On one seemingly ordinary day, I was in a rush to return school rental books. I was trying to get my giant package to fit through the too small slot of the mail bin. I was about to get back in my car and cut my losses when a UPS track pulled up. The UPS driver asked if I wanted him to take the package for me. I quickly said yes and thanked him. As I handed him my box of school books, I couldn't help but feel like I knew him from somewhere. His face…just seemed so oddly familiar, but I couldn't quite put my finger on it. As he drove away, it hit me. It was the original Cody! I quickly realized that two things were very different about him. He was no longer bald and no longer obscenely ripped. No wonder I couldn't place him at first! Never in my wildest dreams did I ever think our paths would cross again. Yet, there we were, several years later.

To Cody:

I couldn't help but wonder if you recognized me. I searched you on Instagram and clicked "follow" just to see if you would say anything. I really didn't want anything to do with you, but my curiosity got the best of me. It didn't take long for you to message me. You told me that you did in fact recognize me. You then proceeded to try to flirt with me. I then took the opportunity to confront you about our past and how you cheated on your girlfriend with me. Only after I brought the subject up, did you apologize. You said that the apology was long overdue and your former girlfriend and me didn't deserve what you did. Let's not fool ourselves though. You're only sorry you got caught. If I had flirted back with you, I would have never gotten that apology. We never spoke again after that. I had the answer to my question. You did recognize me and your appearance was the only thing that had changed.

You played me like a violin,
With grace and expertise.

It sounded sweet as sugar.
You never missed a beat.
Lost in rhythm,
I let you play me.

You played me like a violin,
With grace and expertise.

Even when I snapped,
You kept trying to play.
The sweet music was gone.
It could not be repeated.

You played me like a violin,
With grace and expertise.

So much potential lost.
You played too much.

You played me like a violin,
With grace and expertise.

I no longer attend music class.
Find a new violin to play.

Chapter Four

Fake News

Ever been on a date with a news anchor? How about a guy 17 years older than you? I managed to find a guy with both traits. In this chapter, I will refer to him as Sam. He was tall, had a dazzling smile and piercing blue eyes. You're probably wondering how we met. Unfortunately I can't delve too much into details in order to protect his identity, but sometimes it's not so much about how we meet someone. It's more a matter of what happened next. How did it end? That's what you really need to know.

I gave Sam my phone number and he asked me out on a date. We met up at a cliché coffee spot. Pretty sure we both ordered tea. What was less typical of the date was the fact that we then went to his gym. You're probably thinking "I guess that could be cute, you must have done partner workouts together". That would have been cute. That would have made more sense, but that wasn't the case. We just did our own thing and came together after we were both done with our workout.

To Sam:

You were pretty flirtatious over text message. I couldn't really gauge you though. It appeared you weren't looking for anything serious. Text messages exchanged were inconsistent and sporadic. We would attempt to make plans and you would bail.

More red flags occurred when I noticed you unfollowed me on Instagram. When I confronted you about it, you gave some kind of vague excuse and then followed me back again. Time would pass and once again you would unfollow me on social media. It seemed to be a back and forth pattern. Eventually contact with you seemed to fade out all-together.

You were a very short chapter in my life, but still one I won't easily forget. I remember how star struck I was by the fact that a news anchor took notice of me. To whoever is reading this, this is your reminder not to get distracted by superficial things. Do not be impressed by looks, fame, or fortune. People like that are not meant for you. People like that will never be able to swim the depth of a heart like yours.

Truth be told, it greatly upset me whenever a man walked away from me after I opened up my heart to him. It was disappointing that they were unable to give me the love and commitment I wanted. Now I know that the loss was never mine. They walked away from a woman who would have shown nothing but love and loyalty. So if you walked away from me, I want to thank you. A shallow soul would burn in the depth of a heart as passionate as mine.

-Fake News

I thought you reported what was fact,
But you probably never leave a girl's heart intact.
You were one of those pretty men women rate a ten.
I should have known then, that your departure was just a matter of when.
You seek the next big thing,
Not worrying about leaving a sting.
I saw some signs,
But I'd rather believe your lamentable lines.

Chapter Five

Deleting Facebook is the New Breakup

Growing up, I always loved playing basketball. At one point, I even played on three teams at once. While I was on one of these teams, my coach's nephew seemed to take an interest in me. In this chapter, I will be calling him Scott. We were both probably around 14 at the time, so no major moves were played in the beginning. It would take years for him to shoot his shot.

At the end of my basketball season, my coach threw a party at one of those arcade/sport places that everyone had birthday parties at. My teammates were not the only ones attending. Scott was also there. This is where I really got the inkling he liked me. How could I tell? He acted like any other 14 year old boy with a crush. He stuck to me like glue all night. He wanted to do every game I was playing as well as make sure his shoulder brushed mine whenever possible. Adolescent boys are still learning the art of subtlety.

To Scott:

Some years would pass before we would get into contact again and you would actually shoot your shot. We "dated" briefly in high school, but it wasn't anything too serious. You would even go on to "date" one of my friends! Not too surprisingly, you didn't put much effort into that relationship either. From what I heard, you didn't even see each other!

After about a month of "dating" through text message, you ghosted my friend. This wouldn't be the last time you would break up with someone through your silence.

When I was in college, we actually gave dating a fighting chance, or so I thought. I remember you gave one of your girl cousins my number because you guys were super close and she was very protective of you. Too bad you weren't the one who needed protecting. Even then we didn't see each other much. Red flag alert. The one time I did go to your house I remember meeting your dad. Things seemed to be going decently, but out of the blue I noticed you weren't answering any of my texts. I checked social media and your Facebook was completely gone.

Only when I reached out to Scott's cousin, did I find out what happened. Scott got back with his ex-girlfriend. I couldn't believe it. The audacity of this boy! He didn't even have the courage or enough respect for me to break the news to me. He must have reasoned with himself that ignoring my texts and calls and deleting his Facebook was equivalent to telling me that our relationship was over. *insert face palm emoji*.

Eventually Scott did re-activate his Facebook. Ever since then, he would always try to pop in and out of my life. It was always the same endless pattern. He would say how it's been awhile and ask me how I was. After talking for a bit, he would disappear again. To this day we are still Facebook friends, but things have certainly changed. For one, he has a kid. His kid is pretty cute. I can't lie. However, as Taylor Swift would say, "we are never, ever, getting back together".

"Ghosting"

Now I know why we call it ghosting.
It's because their disappearance haunts you.
You turn over and scrutinize every word and action that occurred,
Wondering what you did to scare them off.
It wasn't you.
They cannot face their own truth.
Their dark souls will rise into the night sky without ever uttering a proper goodbye.
Their minds justify that it is better than telling a lie.
So save yourself the trouble of wondering why.
Don't go searching for him.
His absence no longer needs to haunt you.

Chapter Six

An Unexpected Valentine

One fall, I met a guy who was a manager of an auto repair place, who I will be referring to as John. At the time, I had a boyfriend and he had a girlfriend. Sure, I noticed John was attractive, but my mind never wandered past that. I never viewed him through a romantic lens.

A couple of months went by and I went to the place where he worked since my car was due for maintenance. We chatted briefly. When my car was ready and it was time for me to go, he was nowhere to be found, but I didn't think much of it. However several minutes after I left, I noticed my phone ringing. It was John. He told me that he felt bad that he wasn't around to say goodbye to me. He asked me how I was doing. I admitted to him that I was going through a really hard time because I was about to break up with my boyfriend. He told me that if I ever needed to talk that I could reach out to him.

Again a couple of months go by without any contact. It is now Valentine's Day. Since I am no longer in a relationship, my only plans were to go out to a bar with one of my other single friends later that night. To my surprise, John texted me today of all days. He asked me how I was and if I had any plans. Once I told him my plans, he admitted that he had wanted to take me out to dinner. I told him that since my friend and I weren't going out until after 9 that I could squeeze him in for dinner together. He seemed really excited and even asked me to be his valentine. I can't remember the last time someone asked me that or if anyone had ever asked me that. I thought it was so sweet. I couldn't believe we were going to have our first date ever on Valentine's Day. Not too surprisingly, the sushi restaurant was packed, but neither of us seemed to mind since it just gave us more time to talk.

Since John was taken the last time I had seen/spoken to him, I was genuinely confused that he had wanted to go out with me on this holiday. He told me that they had just broken up a few days prior. WARNING. RED FLAG ALERT. Although I was alarmed with how recently his breakup happened, and rightly so, I tried to brush it off. He explained to me that the relationship died long before he officially ended the relationship.

The next day was a Saturday. We were texting during the day, but didn't have any plans to see each other. He asked if we could meet up, but I told him that I already had plans with one of my best friends. However, as fate would have it, my friend had to cancel because her sister went into labor! What are the odds! So while my friend was on her way to the hospital to become an aunt, I drove to one of my favorite restaurants to meet up with him. It was a really nice night. The conversation flowed easily and we had deep conversations about our past relationships.

John was so enthused by how things were going that he asked me if I would like to go to the movies the next day. Upon my agreement, he even bought the tickets on his phone right then and there. Our next date was already booked. When he walked me to my car, he mentioned that he wanted to kiss me. I told him that we should take it slow. He respected it and we hugged goodbye.

The next day, we met up at the mall to see a movie as planned. During the movie, I could tell John wanted to hold my hand. Me being me, I felt nervous and self-conscious. I felt like my hands were sweating like crazy, but eventually his hand made its way over.

After the movie ended, we decided to grab lunch at the mall and walk around. Once again the conversation flowed very easily between us. We walked around that mall talking for hours. Yet the date still wasn't over. Next we drove to a bar to play some pool. We both had a couple of drinks and the games between us were very close. He would occasionally wrap his arms around me. I couldn't tell if I was more buzzed from the drinks or his presence. By the time he walked me to my car, we had been together for over seven hours! Once again he mentioned how he really wanted to kiss me. This time I let it happen. I felt major sparks kissing him and I knew it was because we were already building a strong emotional bond. I was scared though. I told him that my heart was still healing from my last relationship and I'm not one to half ass anything. I wanted to be able to give him my full heart. He told me he understood.

That night when we were texting he casually slid in the "babe" word. I was surprised that after date three he already wanted to start using cute nicknames, but I went along with it.

John had told me that he would love if I visited him at work so the next day I did just that. He showed me around the store and introduced me to his employees. As I watched him work, it was mesmerizing to watch his eyes change colors when the sun shone through the store window. Sometimes his eyes looked blue. Sometimes they looked green.

The following day, I went to his apartment for the first time. During this visit, I met John's mom and sister. Once we were finally alone, John told me how he couldn't believe how lucky he got. He told me that he was falling for me. The compliments just kept on rolling. He told me how beautiful I am, how I'm probably the most motivated person he knows, how I have a good head on my shoulders, and have a lot going for me between working full time as a therapist and being a published author. What stuck out the most was the fact that he told me that it was not scary for him to fall for me. He said he wasn't afraid because of how amazing I am. He also reassured me that I wasn't a rebound. He told me that he's had rebounds before and that this was completely different. He said that whenever I texted him, he would excitedly answer right away. He continued to explain that if I was a rebound, he would have taken his time getting back to me. You'll see later on how ironic that statement became.

Starting with our first date on Valentine's Day we ended up seeing each other 10 days in a row. During this time, we essentially acted like a couple. We exchanged cute nicknames like babe and we always held hands. In addition to already meeting his sister and mother, I also met his dad. We would go out to eat, play pool at the bar, and go bowling. One night we even went to his friend's house for a small party. I rediscovered my talent for beer pong. John's good friend seemed really happy for him that he met me.

On that 10th day of spending time together, he met my parents and sister, then drove me to the train station for my four day work training in New York. He even offered to pick me up from the station when I came back from my training.

Of course we continued to text every day. There were always good morning and good night texts. I was falling for him hard, but I was still unsure if my heart was completely healed and ready for a new relationship.

However, the more we talked, and the more time we spent together, the more I felt myself healing. I started to truly envision a future with John. We seemed to be building something great. He seemed like a perfect match for me. After all, at this point in time, he seemed to be very driven and hard-working, honest, trustworthy, good at communicating, and someone who believed just as passionately about love and serious relationships as me.

I didn't expect to fall for you like this,
But it all started after that first kiss.
I was so afraid,
But you made the fear start to fade.
I felt stuck in darkness for awhile,
But then you kept making me smile.
My heavy heart had been so full of doubt,
But life has a funny way of working out.
I love being around you,
No matter what we do.
You make my heart race
Whenever I see your face.
I wouldn't mind getting lost with you any place.

After a few weeks of "dating", I noticed another red flag. It seemed minor at the time, but it would later grow in size. One afternoon he texted me once and that was it until the next morning. Now I'm not the kind of girl who needs to talk to her man 24/7. However, I am a huge believer in communication. I would appreciate a heads up if someone is going to be "too busy" to text me for almost twenty-four hours. I explained that to him and he did apologize and said he completely understood. Everything felt right in the world again.

We continued to go on dates and the sparks continued to fly. When we were out, he would randomly kiss my cheeks, forehead, or lips. I felt like I was on cloud nine. One time we even ran into one of his childhood friends and he told me that he had never seen John so happy.

After a month of acting like a couple, I felt like I was ready for the label. After all, we were doing all the things a boyfriend and girlfriend would do. We met each other's family. I met some of his friends. We were very affectionate towards each other and held hands every time we went out somewhere. We talked every day. The only thing missing was an official title. I was excited to tell John that I was ready to fully commit. I was not prepared for the rapid turn of events that would follow.

To John:

The evening I planned to tell you that I was ready to be official was the same night you told me that you were afraid to be in a relationship again. You insisted that you didn't want to hurt me and you didn't want me to hurt you. I felt so blindsided, but you continued to explain that in your past relationships things would start out good and "normal", but then went terribly wrong. You proceeded to tell me that it wasn't like you were seeing someone else or wanted to pursue anyone else. You said how you loved spending time with me. You told me how perfect I am. You insisted that you truly see us being something. The greatest irony was that you also said you didn't want me to feel like you were pushing me away. You explained that you didn't want to see or talk to me any less. You liked how things were. I should have recognized the sign that you just wanted to have your cake and eat it too.

-The questions that haunt her heart

If you can't handle a woman's love,
Why would you drag her from above?
She was flying high,
And now she's asking why
It all feels like a lie.
After three dates, you were already calling her nicknames.
Now it feels like you're just playing games.
She wants to be put first,
To be with someone who accepts her at her worst.
She doesn't want to wait.
By the time you figure life out, it will be too late.
She'll be gone.
She's nobody's pawn.

Of course that was also the night you told me that you wanted to make love to me. I reminded you that we would need to be in an official relationship and in love for that. You made a comment about how it wouldn't take long for you to fall in love with me.

I was really disappointed you weren't ready for a relationship label. However, I tried to be patient and understanding considering that you were right that we both had "recently" gotten out of relationships. It seemed like a valid excuse. It just seemed strange that while I was getting more used to the concept of being a couple, you were becoming more fearful of commitment.

Two weeks after John first admitted his fear of commitment, it was his birthday. He told me how his birthday was never anything special. He told me how he was always let down. I really wanted to show him that it wouldn't be the case with me. I wanted to show him just how much love I have to offer. I bought him a couple of meaningful presents. I bought him his favorite cake. I even wrote him a poem, made him a homemade birthday card, and bought a couple of balloons in his favorite color.

On John's birthday, I went to his work with the balloons, cake, and card in hand. One of his employees made a comment about how sweet the gesture was. I got there at noon and ending up staying until 5:30 when John closed the store. I later drove John to his favorite restaurant to treat him to a birthday dinner.

While I was there, one of John's employees who had an early shift that day called him. To my surprise John repeated the conversation to me and another employee who was hanging out with us at the time. This is what John's employee had to say to him…"We have a saying in my country. Be with the one who wants to be with you and not the one you want to be with. Christine is a very, very, nice girl. Don't f*ck with her head. You two would make a very cute couple".

I didn't think much of it at the time. Looking back now, I wonder why I ran that red light…I shouldn't have overlooked the warning in that statement. Why would his employee say something like that? What was John telling his friends behind closed doors? So many questions I did not consider. I saw flags in John, but just as I always have, I kept chasing after them.

A few days later, John and I were supposed to spend that Thursday and Friday together. Weeks before, we both had taken off work and planned to go out of state to celebrate for his birthday. We were planning to have a spa day at a particular facility and spend the night at a hotel. However, something came up and we decided to skip the out of state venture and just spend the days together in our home state.

On Thursday, we spent the day together as planned. I even attended "family" night with him. I met more members of his family and we all seemed to have a good time. Even in front of his family, John still acted affectionate towards me and referred to me as "babe". He sure put on a good show for a guy afraid of being in a relationship.

That night, he asked again if I wanted to make love and once again I said no. Why do some men expect all the benefits of a girlfriend without the label and commitment?

When we woke up the next morning, he suggested that I go home to get my workout in while he took his friend to the train station and did laundry at his parent's home. I was going to go with him to the train station, but since he mentioned that it would be a good chance for me to get my workout in, I took him up on his offer. It seemed very clear that we would then meet back up after I worked out and he did laundry. After all, some of my things like extra clothes and make-up were still at his place.

Ever since I went home that day, it all drastically went downhill. I got home at 10AM. An hour and a half later, I texted John to let him know I was done with my workout. He didn't answer me until 1PM. He told me that he's "just waiting for laundry to dry". Three hours go by...yes. THREE hours! No response. Now, you and I both know that a standard dryer does not take three hours to dry clothes...I then decide to call John to see what is going on. He didn't pick up the phone and texted me saying that he got a last minute work conference call that would be starting in a few minutes and that he would call me after that.

Finally around five, John called me. I got all choked up and emotional telling him how I didn't feel like a priority and how I had already told him how important communication was to me. He told me that it wasn't true about me not being a priority. He kept apologizing, but it was more of an excuse than an apology. He insisted that he didn't realize we had specific plans to meet up again that day. Mind you, as I mentioned before, we had planned weeks in advance for us to both take off those two days of work to spend extra time together. His "apology"/excuse did not make any sense. My stuff that I needed was still at his place. The exchange during the morning about me only leaving for the sole purpose of getting my workout in did not match his explanation. However, he kept saying he felt terrible and wanted to make it up to me. He asked me if I wanted to "take a step back" and I told him I did. I should have known that his question was actually a projection of his own feelings. Then he told me how you he was going to stay at his parent's house a bit longer and then call me after so I could get my things.

Three hours go by and it is now around 8PM. I decide to text him letting him know that I actually don't want to take a step back. I say that I like how things are, but I just want better communication. No response. I call him at 9:30PM. Still no response. By this time I am fuming. It was so confusing to me for someone to be so seemingly apologetic and repeatedly ask how he can make it up to me and then turn around and do the very same thing he said he would change. He heard how choked up I was over the phone. He knew how upset I was over the poor communication. Why did he insist that I was a priority when I clearly wasn't?

-"Noise"

Even in a quiet place I hear too much noise.
I hear reality knocking on my door.
I hear all the lies crashing through the window.
I hear all the time wasted being blown away by the wind.
I hear it all.
Your voice used to be music.
Your presence used to be a melody worth dancing to,
Your eyes the song worth putting on repeat.
Now you're just noise.

The next morning arrives and I still have not heard from John since our 5PM phone call the night before. I finally call him at 10:30AM. He does not answer. I then promptly text him saying how I need my stuff. Like come on dude! My stuff is there! He then calls me back a minute later. I immediately ask him where he's been. He groggily replies that he got drunk last night. He proceeds to tell me how he drove home drunk around 10:30 at night and passed out. By this point I am so angry, disappointed, and disgusted. I ask him if I can come get my things. As soon as he says yes, I grab my keys and head over to his apartment.

You tried to say you weren't like the rest,
But it seems you've failed the test.

I gave you another shot.
I wasn't asking for a lot.
I just wanted you to communicate,
But you kept making me wait.

To John:

When I got to your place, I tried to tell you off. How dare you leave me on radio silence after knowing how emotional I got over your poor communication? Yet somehow you managed to turn it all around like everything was my fault. You told me that you had warned me that you didn't want to be in a relationship just yet. Oh yeah. A month into acting like a couple. A month after you kept showering me with compliments telling me how I was essentially your dream girl. You definitely gave me plenty of notice and didn't blind side me…You proceeded to tell me how you've always bounced from relationship to relationship, never having time to focus on yourself. You tried to make it seem like you wouldn't be "able to focus on yourself unless we took a step back and became just friends". I tried to explain to you that in a healthy relationship, both partners can still work on themselves. You knew I wasn't the clingy type. You knew I was always okay with you seeing your friends before seeing me. So let's be real. You were just giving me a lame excuse because you didn't know how to be honest with me or yourself. You're the one who started this! You texted me on Valentine's Day. You kept asking to see me. You would text me "I miss you" the same day I saw you. Why did you come on so strong just to back pedal?

-every time you let me down a new poem emerged

Over a month of acting like a couple,
Yet you've left me feeling like the fool.
You said it all happened so fast,
That you're afraid to get hurt like in your past,
But date one you asked me to be your valentine.
Why would you use that line,
If you weren't ready to become mine?
You said I was perfect, but you needed time to focus on you,
But why would you hold my hand and call me boo?
Why did you have me meet your family,
If you weren't ready to give me your heart's key?
I wanted to be all in.
Is that such a sin?
You chipped away at my wall,
Just to not catch me when I would fall.
You've been acting like a clown,
But I wasn't expecting you to let me down.

When I asked John what exactly taking a step back and being "friends" would look like, he explained that we could still text and hangout. I was still welcome to come over to his place any time. He also told me that he realized that his "I'm sorry" was just words, but that he still wanted to prove to me through his actions that he could be better at communicating.

It seemed apparent that we just wouldn't be acting like a couple anymore. I didn't say this to him, but how did he expect me to be okay with going from calling each other "babe", kissing, and hand-holding, to suddenly being just "friends"? If your feelings for me were truly as strong as you displayed the past month and a half, wouldn't that be very difficult for you too?

It's hard to have a heart of gold
In a world so cold.
Always told she's perfect in every way,
But yet they never stay.
They fear her giant heart.
They don't know how to not tear it apart.
They see someone who wants to give them it all.
But yet they stall and build a wall.
Why won't they accept the one who could actually treat them right?
The one who emits light on their darkest night.
They should have held her tight.
For love, she will always fight.

After that conversation, the dynamic of our "relationship" greatly shifted. Contact and communication became even more inconsistent. John would take a day or two to text me back. I couldn't help but think back to his comment about how if I was a rebound he would take his time getting back to me. Despite his minimal efforts, I would always answer him and keep the vicious cycle going.

-"*Caught in a Whirlpool*"

Have you ever made a whirlpool with your friends?
You keep swimming around and around in the pool in the same direction.
After traveling on the same path for a good length of time, you now try to go the other way.
What happens?
You are met with a lot of resistance.
You can feel the weight of the force built from traveling the same direction for so long.
This is like a relationship.

Even if it is toxic and something you should leave behind, when you try to leave, you face resistance.
It is harder to leave a path you are so accustomed to.
It will take time to build enough momentum for you to travel the new direction as comfortably as you did the previous one.
I was caught in your whirlpool.
I did not have the strength to swim the other way just yet.

To John:

You were right about one thing. Words are just words. As a writer, I strongly believe in the power of words, but sadly, not everyone practices what they preach. Your actions were telling me everything I needed to know. It was time to stop ignoring your red flags. You had shown me time after time, that you didn't value me or my time. You came and went as you pleased. You only talked to me when it suited your mood. I knew all along that I deserved so much better than that.

-You still cross my mind

Sometimes I wonder if the birthday card I made you still hangs on your office wall.
Maybe you're waiting for it to fall.
What about the poem I wrote you?
Probably in a corner collecting dust.
Was your heart only full of lust?

-I grew up playing with red flags

You remind me of someone I once knew.
He also started out too good to be true.
You both even had the same hypnotic eyes that fed me lies.

Am I that drawn to capture flags?
Like damn.
I know I was good and always wanted to play in gym class,
But now I'd like to pass.

-Darling, you were never asking for too much

When his waves pull towards your shore,
I hope you don't chase them anymore.
He was no prince with a crown.
He will only watch you drown.
Don't offer him a hand,
Just let his waves stumble upon the sand.
It's time to walk away from the one who was never going to stay.

-You were too weak to carry a heart like hers

You told me I wasn't a rebound,
But now you're barely around.
Why did you call me babe after date three,
When you weren't really serious about me?
You jumped the gun.
Yet just as quickly wanted to be done.
Maybe it was all too good to be true.
Now you're just a stranger I once knew.

-The irony of it all

The irony is that you helped heal my heart,
Just to tear it apart.
I was just getting over heartbreak.
There's only so much a girl can take.
I feel lost again.
I don't understand men.
They say all the right things for awhile,
Knowing just how to make you smile.
They tell you you're amazing in every way,
Yet their actions don't match what they say.
They leave you like you hadn't spent the past month talking every day.
Now my heart has to pay.

"Lost Treasure"

Rain falls relentlessly from above,
Each drop accumulating into a depth I once dove head first into.
When my heart and head hit the water,
They let the ocean consume them,
But my head came up for air,
It learned the difference between sacrifice and suffocation.
My heart still swam until it finally fell to the ocean floor.
Bursts of bubbles surrounded it.
Despite the pressure pulling it under,
It kept rising.
Who knew all those treacherous swim lessons would pay off.
Fear is not the enemy.
Sinking does not kill,
Only sitting still.
Rise above your fears.
Rise above the depth they dug and left you to be buried in as if you were fool's gold.
Only a true fool buries a heart of gold.

One more deserving will find and cherish what they left behind.
They'll come back looking for the treasure they threw to sea,
But they will never find you.
You've risen into all they thought you could never be.

"Just a Dream"

The more time that passes,
The more you feel like a distant memory.
Nothing more than a dream I had to wake up from,
But the ending never sat well with me.
We like happy endings.
We like clear cut answers.
But more often than not, things happen and change mid-sentence.
We wake up in the middle of a dream.
We wake up sometimes just to drift back into unconsciousness.
You were the star of my dreams once upon a time,
But the show is over.
You don't light up my night sky anymore.
I feared no one would again,
But you led me to a new star,
One that shines brighter than all the rest I've ever encountered.
I am lucky to have found a shooting star that stays.

-He was the sun

I was always chasing the sun,
Hoping to capture some of its light,
But time and time again, it would dip below the sky and seem out of reach.
Then one day, I stopped chasing.
I realized I had the light inside me all along.
I just had to set it free.
I had to set myself free.

Chapter Seven

Diamond in the Rough

This chapter will be about a man I will refer to as Jeremy. Jeremy and I have been friends on Instagram for a few years. I don't even remember how that even happened. All I know is that we've been "social media friends" for quite some time. Throughout the years, we've been in contact on and off, commenting on each other's Instagram stories. We even tried to make plans to meet in person, but something always seemed to come up.

However, we did eventually FaceTime for the first time. Our contact in general became more constant. We started texting each other every day. I began to realize more and more how much we had in common. We both identify as Catholic and believe in God. We are both certified trainers and committed to fitness. We both enjoy exchanging corny jokes and puns. We even share some of the same favorite country artists.

Although Jeremy is a year younger than me, he seemed to be an old soul. He appeared to be a hopeless romantic like me. He was also super close with his family and loved dogs. He was ambitious and hard working. While working three jobs, he was going to school to get his doctorate in physical therapy. It seemed like he was checking off all the right boxes. Could it be possible that I actually found an attractive man who was entirely compatible with me who also sought a serious relationship? Was I overlooking a diamond in the rough on Instagram all these years?

"A Diamond in the Rough"

Maybe the timing was never right before,
But now my heart and head are no longer at war.
I was so busy collecting stones in the caves,
I didn't notice the sparkling glow underneath the waves.
The stones would always skip smoothly at first,
But would ultimately sink down under.
It would start to thunder and I would wonder why.
I should have known men of stone will only make you feel alone.
I finally took notice of the sparkle beneath the murky water.
I would have been a fool to not choose this priceless jewel.
Maybe love won't be as tough,
With a diamond from the rough.

Six weeks of texting every day went by, but it felt as if our "relationship" was at a standstill. We had not met each other in person yet, but that wasn't too surprising given the COVID-19 situation. However, I was hoping that we would at least be talking on the phone and Facetiming often to build our emotional connection.

When we first started texting each other consistently, we did have a few Facetime conversations. Then a month went by where texting is our only means of communication. I brought up Facetime quite a few times, but he never acted on it.

Honestly, our dynamic was confusing to me. Here we were exchanging text messages every day, but flirting seemed to be minimal. Whatever kind of relationship we had seemed to be leaning towards the friend zone.

I believe in passion. I want a love that ignites my heart on fire. I would rather risk being burned, than not feel the warmth of passion.

Jeremy seemed like a genuine guy, but even after "talking" consistently for 6 weeks, he was hard to read. I just knew in my heart that it was time to move on. It was a shame, considering all the things we had in common, but he was lacking the initiative and effort I sought. Texting is not enough to build a meaningful connection. Call me. Facetime me. Ask me deep questions. I'm tired of short lived small talk.

However, I tried to give him one last chance. I brought up Facetime yet again and he once again put me off. Apparently painting his room was a bigger priority. Eventually he stopped texting me. I'm sure if I texted him, he would have answered, but it most likely would have initiated another dead end cycle.

To Jeremy:

It was also off putting that after not talking for a couple of days, you mentioned how you "had been dealing with stuff" and like to do it yourself. You didn't elaborate any further. I understand sometimes we need space to figure out things ourselves, but I at least want my partner to be less vague about what he is going through. For claiming to be an open book, you seemed closed off to me. That was another indication that we would not be a good match.

-She was the book you should have finished

I'm the book they want to open.
They see the pretty pictures.
They skip the somber lines.
They seek the somatic surface.
They disregard the scarred pages.
I'm the book they want to open.
They read what's relevant to them.
They rip out what they want to know.
They miss the book's true message.
They never discover its true value.
I'm the book they want to open,
But never finish.

Conclusion

Looking back, I often ask myself why I ignored so many red flags. Why did I give men chance after chance? I'm sure most people would consider a second chance generous. I think I usually would call it quits after the 95,482,284th chance. I mean, these men could be waving several damn flags in my face and I would still question my own gut! I could have all the evidence stacked against them, and I would still struggle to not give them the benefit of the doubt. I would tell myself, "Maybe I'm overreacting. There's no way they could do that to me. They're truly sorry. They'll change this time".

You see, people with big hearts can't help but view the world through their rose colored glasses. No matter how many times people let them down and reveal their true colors, they still hold on to the belief that people are capable of change. We see the potential in people. We know that people are not simply all "good" or "bad". We know that humans are so much more complex than that.

Many people see this as a weakness, and in certain ways, it is. Our big hearts put us at a greater risk for deception. Our hearts are more likely to fall victim to manipulation and abuse. We put up with a lot more than we should. We put a lot of time and effort into people who are incapable of reciprocation.

However, I wouldn't change a thing because it is also a strength. Just as the abusers' actions reveal who they truly are, our actions reveal who we truly are. We may be guilty of overlooking red flags, but at least our intentions are pure.

Our loyalty is undeniable. Our big hearts allow us to love deeply. It is why we always make time for you. It is why we don't make you chase after our love. You see, we would rather drown in love, than be deprived of it. We are not afraid to feel, and that's what makes us real.

They are drawn to her ocean,
But fear drowning in her love.
They'd rather say their goodbyes than
Face the storm in her eyes.
They didn't realize that it is better to risk pain.
All those swimming lessons they took in vain.

If I have learned anything from these experiences, it is this. There comes a time when you have to take off your rose colored glasses and accept reality. You have to stop questioning yourself. Yes, sometimes people deserve a second chance. Yes, sometimes people do truly change. However, it is important to distinguish the difference. I'm not saying I have a fool-proof plan because that just isn't possible. There is always a risk when it comes to dating and love. I will review with you the red flags I have noticed in my own life. Then you will have to judge for yourself if that flag is worth catching.

Red Flag #1: They bail on plans. Of course life happens. Things come up. However, beware if they seem to make a habit of canceling plans at the last minute.

Red Flag #2: There is a lack of communication. They will always randomly stop texting you. Maybe even text you back a day or two later. Most of us have jobs and very hectic schedules, but it only takes a minute to let someone know you're unavailable. Their ability to communicate with you will also show you how big a priority you are in their lives. We MAKE time for what matters to us. Don't let them make you think otherwise.

Red Flag #3: They never post you on social media. I understand some people like to keep their personal lives private, but I think we can all agree that if they can't post a single picture of you, there should be some alarm bells going off.

Red Flag #4: Their actions don't match their words. They apologize for something, but then continue to do the very thing they apologized for. There is no change in behavior. That is not a real apology. That is manipulation.

Red Flag #5: You know they have a significant other, but they try to flirt with you. They compliment your appearance. A person who cheats on their partner (whether it is emotional or physical) will most likely do the same thing to you if given the chance.

Red Flag #6: They lie to you. I'm not talking about the little white lies we say to spare each other's feelings at times. I'm talking about lying about important matters. You found out they were not at the place they said they would be. You found out that their substance use addiction has been continuing without your knowledge. When heavy lies get involved, trust is broken. Without trust, how can a relationship survive and flourish? If they can lie about one thing, it makes it all the more easy for them to lie about other things.

Red Flag#7: They are more interested in staying in with you than taking you out somewhere in public in the beginning of your "relationship". Lustful people do not value you. They are not interested in getting to know your emotional heart. They might also have other ulterior motives and not want others to view them as off the market.

Red Flag #8: They come on VERY strong. Now I often say that I "fall hard and fast" myself, but I'm talking about when someone starts telling you that that they picked out your wedding song after a few days of texting. When someone starts showering you with compliments right off the bat it does not carry as much value as it would after you have been spending more time together in person. Most people know all the right things to say. Observe if their actions match.

Red Flag #9: They are VERY protective of their phone. They never leave it behind. If they do even leave their phone in the room with you it is passcode protected and/or turned upside down. They never ask you to answer their phone for them or hand it to them. I'm not saying partners should look through each other's phone or feel the need to, but why would someone act so secretive and protective if they didn't have something to hide...

Red Flag #10: They show lack of trust in you. They question your loyalty. Many times the ones accusing are the ones cheating. They are projecting their own actions onto you. Even if they are not cheating, how can you be in a healthy relationship with someone who doesn't trust you? Lack of trust puts a lot of strain on the relationship and never ends well.

Red Flag #11: They say you deserve better or they are worried they are not good enough for you. Every man who ever said these words to me always turned out to be right. When someone makes a comment like that, it is an early warning sign that they are not the right match for you. If you hear the words "you deserve better" or "I don't think I'm good enough for you", run. They know they have the potential to harm you, psychologically or physically. They know the truth...you deserve better.

I also want to note that sometimes red flags can remain hidden for a good length of time. In other words, people can put up a good front in the beginning. They will try to hide their red flags from view. You see, these people can typically keep up their "good behavior" for the first 4-5 months. After that, their true colors will emerge. They're hoping that by now you've developed a secure attachment and deep feelings for them. They know it is a lot harder to run from flags when you're emotionally invested.

Sometimes their plan works. The red flags start popping up, but you've already put on your rose colored glasses. You notice something is off, but you can't quite put your finger on it. Maybe you start having some doubts, but you quickly push them aside. This person has been nothing but sweet and amazing to you the past few months. You cling to that view of them.

I think that is what scares a lot of people including myself about relationships. Everyone is familiar with the beginning "honeymoon" stage of a relationship. Everything is perfect. You seemed to have found that one special person who shares all the same values as you. All the stars seem aligned. The scary part is that many people do not reveal their whole true self until after 4-5 months.

I challenge you to take the risk. Take the risk for love. However, heed my warning. After 4-5 months pass, I hope you take off your rose colored glasses. Even if you just take them off long enough to notice the red flags. I hope you don't brush them off and ignore them. If he runs, don't chase him. Take it from me. He is not the red flag you want to capture.

"You Cannot Gain Without Some Pain"

There are days I sink so deeply into my thoughts I find myself drowning.
I envision splendid sparkling sunlight shining above the surface,
But it is hard to swim through my murky mind,
But even through the dark,
A seashell glows,
Illuminating the sea in hues of blue, purple, and pink,
Because beauty can reach the bottom of despair,
Even if it seems rare.
Someone, somewhere will care.
But cruelty also hides out there.
Once warm waters can turn ice cold.
A frozen beating heart searching for warmth,
But consumed by ice,
But maybe the words that swim instead of sink will reach it.
It could take days, weeks, or years,
But I'll find a reason to smile through the tears,
Because I believe in something.
A shooting star was reflected in the ice one dark night,
Blinding me briefly with its brilliance.
Even though it left as abruptly as it came,
It ingrained my soul with shapes of sorts,
Shattering who I was and what I thought I knew.
Renewing my hope that I can start again.
I can find myself again.
The sky isn't the limit.
I can go farther.
Greater things can't be seen.
They can only be felt,
And isn't that the most beautiful pain there is?
To feel it all so intensely shooting through your veins,
Burning as bright as the scorching summer sun,
Like a fire dancing in the night,
Hurts to touch, but mesmerizing all the same.
You cannot gain without some pain.

"Old Soul"

I am an old soul.

I believe in quality over quantity.

I want to gaze at a sky frosted with shining stars and talk about why you never leave the house without that locket.

Tell me what scares you the most.

Tell me what goes through your mind when the sky lights up with shades of pink and violet or shimmering yellow and eccentric orange.

I see and value the beauty of words, of voices, of truth, of nature, of silence.

I see and value the beauty of people who not only dream of the potential I am capable of, but accept and cherish the reality of who I am currently.

Having a big heart is a double edged sword.

You have the gift of compassion and empathy.

People want to feel understood and when you can empathize you don't just feel bad for someone's hardships, you actually feel their pain.

You know what it's like to be in that person's shoes and experience what they are experiencing.

Yes having a big heart means you feel much more than the average person.

It can be cut more easily by the sharp edge of the sword,

BUT its capacity for love is relentless.

It will grow and endure.

It repairs itself and tries again.

It will keep searching until it finds another like-minded soul.

Physical attraction temporarily draws people together.

Add a mental connection and they are together until they die.

Give me a physical, mental, and soul connection.

With these three components, I know we shall live forever.

When our bodies catch up in age to our minds, our souls will drift away together into the unknown because there will always be more questions than answers,

But how dull would it be to know the answer to everything?

"Collection"

Back in the day I used to collect little things,
Like those tiny bouncy balls that flew through the halls and down the street.
I used to collect stuffed animals you could play and cuddle with.
I used to collect those Pokemon cards everyone had to have.
Now it's 2020,
And I still collect.
I collect memories;
Those moments that changed your life forever,
For better or worse,
That made you who you are today,
Those moments that marked the blank canvas of your soul,
Those moments that left intangible scars along your skin.
Those moments that ignite a flame inside or freeze your heart to the point
of despair.
I am a collection.
I am not my past.
I am not my present.
I am not my future.
I am a collection of my past, present, and future.
Directly or indirectly, I am shaped every day by my own choices and the
choices of others around me.
I am a collection of colors;
Red as brilliant as boiling blood;
Black as dark as a vacant night sky.
Maybe I've always had kaleidoscope eyes,
Seeing all sorts of colors and shapes.
Do you understand my collection?
We might collect different things, but at the end of the day,
We all collected something,
And that is another page of a book we have yet to finish.

CPSIA information can be obtained
at www.ICGtesting.com
Printed in the USA
BVHW031054260620
582396BV00004B/32/J